From the Team at Abluze Media

The Ultimate Guide
for
Small Business Digital Marketing

Print Edition
by Mark Stafford

https://warner.house

Published by Warner House Press of Albertville, Alabama, USA

Warner House Press
1325 Lane Switch Road
Albertville, AL 35951

Published 2022

S26 25 24 23 22 1 2 3 4 5

ISBN: 978-1-951890-46-9

Table of Contents

Section 1: Overview and Introduction

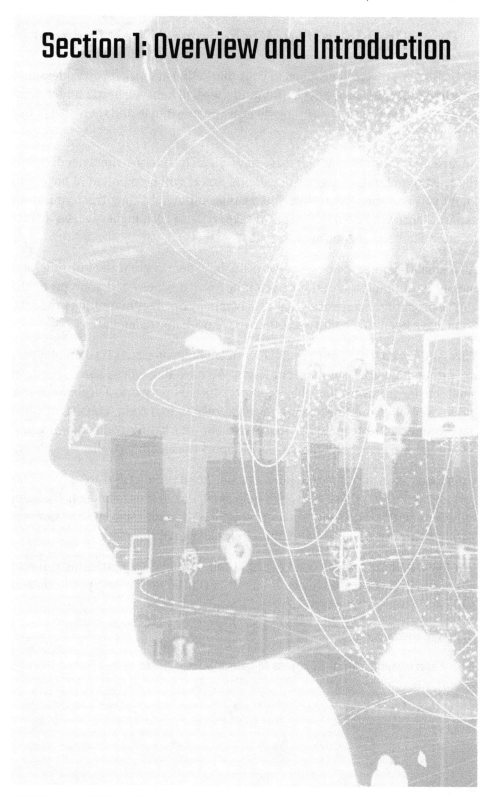

Drive People to Your Website and Then Engage!

Websites are powerful weapons in your marketing arsenal, if you understand how to utilize them properly! In this guide, we will help you better understand how to develop your website, how to draw people into it, and then how to use it to drive sales.

Advertising alone isn't enough these days. Small business owners need to earn the trust of potential buyers. Your digital assets will help potential buyers to know you and then get to like you so that, ultimately, they trust you as an expert. Those who earn the status of "expert" also earn higher wages, attract a better clientele, and make more sales.

As a small business owner, you've probably spent a great deal of time and money developing a website to promote your business and your products. You've probably also spent a great deal of money on other marketing products. Some have been successful and others have probably fallen flat.

This guide is based on our research with small businesses (1-10 employees) operating in a variety of different fields. We have discovered some trends in small business advertising that seem to consistently work. Throughout this guide, we will sometimes compare those results to a train. Consistently, we have found some techniques that drive the marketing train forward and additional marketing techniques that support those efforts well.

Used together in harmony and put alongside great product and great customer service, we've seen these strategies help small businesses to take off. BUT...let me offer you this warning: used improperly, we've also seen small businesses waste thousands of dollars and ultimately close their doors.

Just like a hammer can be used to either build or destroy, marketing can also be used to build or to destroy your business. Our hope is to help you build and build and build some more!

Here's to more customers!

-The Ablaze Media Small Business Marketing Specialists

Maximizing the 20% of Advertising Opportunities That Actually Work

Small business owners run up against this advertising problem all the time: They are bombarded with account executives who promise that their publication, website, radio station, or digital marketing service is the one that will be the magic bullet that drives customers to a business.

Over time, many small business owners become frustrated with their efforts. 80% of media purchases don't seem to be bringing clients into the door. In this guide, we want to identify the 20% that work for most small businesses and then help you understand how to use those tools most effectively.

The 20%

Which ad buys and marketing products actually work for small businesses? We have been doing a fair share of research to come up with an answer to that 20% question. What if a small business could spend most of their ad budget on the 20% that works?

Recent studies show that a cross-platform campaign strategy is deadly effective. Print is by no means dead and digital is not the only way to go.

Things have changed and strategies have had to adapt. Print has moved over to make room for the explosive rise of digital media and, the truth is, digital media has some huge benefits. So, throughout this guide, we are going to talk largely about online or digital strategies while helping you understand how to leverage print assets as well.

Why does digital media work for small businesses so well?

- It is inexpensive
- It is exact
- It is interactive

The downside of digital media? **It can also feel cheap and temporary.** Sometimes it can come across as annoying if it is used improperly and can damage your business. So, let's talk about how to use it well! But first, some research:

Studies about the effectiveness of print:

A few years back, Neilson did a study that looked at the retail sector to see how US consumers arrived at a purchasing decision. The results were astounding in this digital age. Believe it or not, more than half of the consumers surveyed said that they were more persuaded by printed circulars and direct mail than by digital ads. We will suggest throughout this guide that, in the long run, pay-per-click ads are not as effective as email and content marketing (with good social media cross-posting and proper SEO programming).

Further, the leading metric for digital advertising was not social media ad buys or pay-per-click, as you might expect, but a well-written, old-fashioned email campaign followed up by a great website.

What can we learn from these studies?

- None of the studies suggest that you should abandon your print marketing strategy for the sake of digital ads. You should change them, but not abandon them. We suggest that print ads are most effective when they are linked to your internet assets.

- Your small business needs an effective printed advertising method and a great email marketing plan supported by a professional website.

Let's Picture Your Marketing Strategy as a Train

The tracks the train sits on are your company's branding. Your branding is important and you should not start a marketing campaign until your brand is put together properly. Later in this guide, we'll touch on how to properly put your brand together. If you don't have a logo, a basic visual identity for your business, and basic signage, then you're not quite ready to start advertising yet.

Marketing is about getting people to look for you in the first place. Our research shows us that a large percentage of what is working right now for small businesses also happens to be three of the least-expensive media pieces to develop:

Print, Email, and Web

These are the main engines that drive most effective small business marketing campaigns.

Let's unpack them a little right now and, later in the guide, we'll go into much greater detail

Your Website: Your Home

The home of your brand and your marketing efforts is your website. If you are taking your marketing seriously, your website should look professional. It needs to be easy to navigate, rich in content, and maintained often. WordPress is currently the preferred platform for most small business websites.

Something in print:

Research is still showing that direct mail, circulars, postcards, magazine ads, and printed newsletters are hugely effective if they are done properly. So, pick one well-written, well-designed print piece that is delivered to your target demographic at least once per month. Change the artwork monthly. Offer a new, limited-time monthly special. Depending on your industry, these print publications could be:

- Postcards, direct mail, or EDDM
- Circular or coupon mailers
- Glossy local or trade magazines
- Newspapers or newsletters
- Custom greeting cards sent out by a greeting card service.

Don't try something just once. Commit to it for at least six months and then evaluate its effectiveness.

Email marketing:

Lastly, develop an email campaign that follows up with new clients and re-targets existing clients in order to invite them back to the business to make more purchases.

- Mailchimp is an easy-to-use and affordable tool for getting this done.
- Some credit card processors offer a free email retargeting service as well.

If web, print and email aren't covered, there is no reason to move on to other, alternative methods of advertising. For some small businesses, especially owner-operators, this could be all the marketing you'll need to keep yourself booked.

Later in the guide, we'll move onto more complicated media types, like content marketing, pay-per-click, broadcasting, and so on. First, let me offer a few words about how to make just your print, web and email pieces work together for you. Here are a few helpful techniques to drive and track customers from print to digital and vice-versa:

#1: Track It

You need to know if you have an underperforming ad. If so, it is either because you are using the wrong media or because you have the wrong content. Either way, you need to know if you are getting visitors from your advertisements, so make sure to embed a way to track traffic from your print ads.

We suggest to, in your print advertising, use a URL that is unique to that advertisement (and which forwards to your main site) or use a unique phone number that you are able to track. If you don't get clicks or calls, DROP IT! Most of our clients want to see at least $3–4 in profit for every dollar they spend on an advertisement. Unless you build in a way to track, you'll never know if the advertisement is working.

#2: Combine Direct Mail with Online Content

Used together, direct mail and digital can play to each other's strengths.

- Digital options provide immediacy and a modern edge that print can't offer.
- Print provides a level of trust and stability that digital can't offer. Additionally, direct mail lasts longer. It is often left sitting on a counter or a desk for much longer than a digital ad or an email is left on someone's computer screen. Remember, direct mail does not face junk filters or unsubscribe buttons and it doesn't require anyone to opt in.

When a message is coordinated across your digital and print platforms, it can give your digital advertising a seemingly longer shelf life. We'll talk more about effective print strategies later in this guide.

#3: Use Direct Mail to Direct People to Your Website

Recent studies have shown that direct mail will drive more traffic to a website than social media, if readers are asked to visit a website by the print collateral.

In our experience, we almost always see a direct correlation between a spike in website traffic and a well-designed print piece that directs people to visit that website.

Make your website robust, easy to navigate, and full of useful information. Later in the guide, we'll discuss more about good website design and content. Then, use your print pieces to direct people to the great content on your site. On your site, make a great offer that requires people to enter in an email address to receive. This powerful combination gives you the opportunity to retarget those leads through a high-impact email campaign later.

#4: Don't Just Raise Awareness

Always include a call to action on every advertisement. **Advertising is too expensive to be passive.** An advertisement is a waste of money if it is designed primarily to spread awareness of your logo. I'm a huge advocate of ditching logo awareness campaigns. Small businesses need to sell and advertisements that sell always have a clear call to action.

- If you want them to come to the store, invite them.
- If you want them to take advantage of a sale, ask them to buy.

When designing a print piece, ask yourself: "What do I want people to do when they see this ad?" People read about seven words, they look at pictures, and they might take one action. DON'T WASTE YOUR AD by making the call to action unclear.

Blog posts on your website and expert articles in journals or trade magazines are proper places to develop your brand depth and establish yourself as an expert. A print ad is not the place for passive content, massive logos, or expert articles. Print advertising is for selling a product in seven words or less with a great picture. We'll talk more about effective advertising design later in this guide.

#5: Coordinate Your Efforts

Later in this guide, I'll touch on social media and a number of other advertising avenues. As your organization grows, you could find yourself with a dozen different account executives working for a dozen different media organizations. Plus, you may have multiple designers and producers. They will never naturally be on the same page.

You need to coordinate your advertising efforts on a regular basis. Have regular creative meetings so your media staff all remain on the same page.

Managing two or three media organizations is not too difficult. If you have more than a few media organizations to manage, it might be time to hire an advertising agency. They will help you to evaluate the effectiveness of campaigns, help to negotiate contracts, and typically have reliable sources for design, copywriting, and production services.

Matching the Right Type of Media to Your Preferred Clientele

Every legitimate media outlet has a very specific target audience.
Here's what I mean:

- A magazine knows who their readers are.
- A radio station knows their listeners.
- A 24-hour news station knows who is watching.

Media organizations are put together to appeal to certain types of people whom advertisers often want to target. It's all very intentional. As a small business owner, you should be aware of your target audience so that you know how to best spend your advertising dollars.

A good media organization never tries to be all things to all people. An advertising executive who tries to tell you otherwise is simply not being truthful. Every media outlet has a very specific group of people, purpose, demographic, income bracket, and/or geographic area in mind. Your small business should also have a target audience in mind. Make sure your target demographic matches up with the outlet's.

If Your Business Does Not Define a Target Audience, Your Advertisements Will Not Usually Hit the Right People

If a small business doesn't intentionally market to their ideal client, they will usually market to the owner instead. Sometimes, the owner happens to be their ideal client as well, but usually that's not the case, so the target audience needs to be well-defined so you don't waste your money!

When we ask business owners to describe their target audience, four out of five times, the business owner will say something like, "We have all kinds of people come into our store." That is probably true, but not everyone who comes into your shop is an ideal client. The only organization that truly does not have a target audience is the IRS. Everybody else has a type of client that works best for their business.

No matter if you are a manufacturer, a non-profit, a skilled laborer, or a banker, there is a type of person who fits best with your type of business, who often becomes a repeat customer, and who is satisfying to work with.

You need to design the imaging for your business or product with that target audience in mind.

Small businesses who don't identify this person very specifically will typically put together marketing collateral that the owner likes instead of what attracts their very best client.

So, let me give you a couple of tips for identifying your target audience:

#1: Look at your last five sales and ask:

- What is their gender?
- What is their age? (For example: child, teen, young adult, middle aged, retiree)
- Are they clearly part of a subculture that you can identify? (Like homeowner, golfer, artist, manager, laborer, etc)
- How much did they spend? (Was it profitable enough to do again?)
- Did you like **working** with them?

If you made a profit, liked the client, and would like to work with them again, then take note of their age, subculture and gender. This could be a great target audience.

#2: Look at your five best clients and ask the same questions:

- What is their gender?
- What is their age?
- Are they clearly part of a subculture that you can identify?
- How much did they spend? (Was it profitable enough to do again?)

Often your five favorite clients share traits with the last five sales you made. See what lines up and what doesn't. The overlapping qualities may further define your target audience.

Assess:

Then, you need to ask: is your current audience the one you're shooting for? Are they the people you'd like to be working with in five years? If not, what needs to change in your advertisement to attract the right type of customer to your shop?

One of my clients spent a great deal of time developing a target audience for their product. They identified their target audience as:

- A white, 44-year-old woman
- Married with three kids: one teen from a previous marriage and two elementary-aged kids
- Religious, church-going
- Upper-middle income

They even put a picture up of her so they would be reminded all the time to target her and not anyone else.

Typical Audiences for Most Local Media

We believe that a website, a regular targeted print piece, and email are usually the three best marketing pieces to begin with. In reality, the three promotional products that are most commonly utilized by local small businesses are print, radio, and social media ads. Are these the best options for you?

A good website and email marketing strategy are critical before you start with anything else. **Print, radio, and social media should all point back to your website!**

However, local advertising salespeople can be really convincing. *(I used to be one of them.)* Let me share with you what actually works for local businesses when it comes to these local options. Here are the typical audiences for those media types:

Typical print media choices in each market:

Let's start with print. Our experience is that a regular print piece is helpful for most businesses if it is written and designed well. Keep in mind that an ad listing out all your services in tiny print will usually get ignored. Effective print advertisements need to be large, they need faces of people (not work trucks), and ad copy that sells a product in about 7 words. **YOU NEED TO WRITE YOUR AD COPY CAREFULLY!** In most markets, there are these three print media types:

- **The local print newspaper and the Yellow Pages**: Both publications have almost the exact same audience. People who still get paper delivery or who still use the yellow pages are typically older. They tend to be baby boomers and upper-middle class. There is a good percentage of male readers. Ads can be effective AS LONG AS THE TYPE IS REALLY BIG and there is a lot of white space.
  (Doctor's offices, hearing aid companies, pharmacies, grocery stores, luxury car dealerships, country clubs, and premium residential services are often successful in newspapers and Yellow Pages ads.)

- **Neighborhood coupon mailer:** These booklets often go out in the tens of thousands and they are usually picked up by bargain hunters. They can be incredibly effective if you have a sale on a product that costs $100 or less. If you offer premium services, then these mailers can clog up your phone lines with people who have no intention of buying. *(Haircutting franchises, car washes, dollar stores, discount clothing stores, and pizza restaurants often do well in coupon mailers.)*

- **Neighborhood magazine:** Our experience is that these target homeowners, who are typically female in very specific higher-end neighborhoods (with very specific and easily identifiable needs). They are typically effective for people offering higher-end residential services. *(Window washing, water delivery, handymen, vets, remodeling, and house cleaners might be successful in the neighborhood magazine.)*

Local radio advertising:

Local radio can also be an effective medium, if used properly. The daily news and the local information the radio provides still make it widely listened to—especially with adults over the age of 40. Radio creates theater of the mind. Listing off services without emotion gets lost in the noise. Creating an experience with sound effects, storytelling, and word pictures can make an advertisement that is more effective than television at a fraction of the price.

YOU WILL NEED TO SCRIPT THE AD CAREFULLY! Account executives are usually overworked and radio producers are often working for multiple stations as well as doubling as on-air talent. It is typically account executives or producers who get tasked with writing ad copy. They just want to make the sale and get it on their air. You'll have to insist on an engaging and creative script or they will write whatever is easiest to write.

There are three different radio types that are common in most markets:

- **Political talk radio** is radio with active listeners. It is not just music in the background (like the easy listening station). Talk radio listeners turn it up and listen to it passionately. These stations are typically right-leaning and political in nature. Their average listener is usually male and over 55. Companies with products that appeal to older, conservative men often are successful with talk radio. (Dress shirts, grooming products, luxury cars, pickup trucks, tools, etc.)

- **NPR** is similar demographically to a typical talk radio station, but leans to the left politically and has a larger female audience. NPR is also non-profit and they are not allowed to give a call to action. In other words, they can give facts about your business, but they cannot tell people what to do with those facts. Most small businesses with limited budgets are better served by commercial stations that allow a direct call to action during the advertisement.

- **The religious music station** also has a similar audience, but tends to have more female listeners and advertising on this station is usually only effective for companies with the same religious values as the listening audience.

- **Contemporary Country** is widely listened to and wildly popular. Most are surprised to learn that most country listeners are mostly female. 65% of country radio listeners are 35- 55 year old women. They are listening in their cars and if you own a car lot, an auto detailing company, or a drive-thru restaurant, this is a great fit.

- **The top 40 or Adult Contemporary station** also has a mostly female audience. It is largely moms in minivans who are too distracted to bother with hooking up the phone to the Bluetooth. She likes the music, the kids like the music...good enough. Let's go to soccer practice. Family-oriented companies do well with these stations. (Dentists, pediatricians, pizza, mini golf, movie theaters, etc.)

A note about social media:

Social media is highly effective, easy to track, and organic search results are a major sales funnel for nearly every small business we talk with.

A good social media and SEO team using proper programming, content marketing, and paid social media buys can zero-in on a target audience quite effectively. A great website helps convert sales as well. We will talk about website content and social media extensively later in this guide.

A Case Study

Based on this data, let's say you're opening a new Supercuts franchise. First, get the basics done: a good logo and brand identity with a good website and email marketing strategy. A haircutting franchise has a pretty clear target audience. You would be looking for a middle-class, middle-income woman with kids. You would probably want to consider these advertising products:

1. Targeted social media ads with a coupon offer

2. Radio spots on the Adult Contemporary radio station

3. Coupon mailer with a special, limited-time offer

4. Great signage at your retail location

Using Local Business Listings to Attract New Customers

Small businesses often rely on local business listings and local traffic to drive sales. I have had clients talk to us about building a website for them before they have taken even the basic step of adding their business to Google My Business. Without some basic business listings, your business will be really difficult to find online—even if you have a terrific website!

Local business listings are a great way for your business to be found online. The marketplace is crowded and you need to take advantage of every opportunity to get found! Joining a business listing site is like displaying your business card on a billboard. It will help to expand your reach to a wider audience. Local business listings help potential customers find you who would not otherwise do so.

Some Are Free. Some Aren't. Here's When to Pay:

The benefit of using a listing service is that it heightens your visibility among those people who typically rely on such pages for referrals. These listings can also help your business get noticed if it is in a niche industry.

There are free listing services online, like Google My Business, that every small business should take advantage of. **Don't do anything else until you've listed your business with Google!** There are some listing services pages like Yelp, Alignable, and Next Door which offer free accounts. Social media platforms rank well in search results and opening a business page on a platform like Facebook can also help your business to get found online.

So, When Do You Pay?

You start paying when that platform can put you in front of your target audience more effectively. For example, paying for a Chamber of Commerce membership and establishing a listing on their website is really effective for a business that markets to other businesses.

I once was contacted by a company which makes specialty brackets for professional audio system installations. A listing in the local Chamber of Commerce probably would not have helped them, but a listing in a professional audio service directory would be valuable and worth paying for.

Consider Upping Your Game If You Need to Reach Out Further

Restaurants:

Some of the heaviest local internet traffic we've seen has been for restaurants. People search online to look at food, reviews, menus, and so on. The restaurant space is really crowded online. If you're wanting to stand out online, then you're probably going to need to pay for some directory listings.

For restaurants, there are a number of well-established online directories and reservation services like OpenTable.com.

Home improvement:

This is another competitive industry. We build websites for contractors all the time, but the most successful contractors online combine directory listings, social media posts, paid advertising, and content marketing. Lists like HomeAdvisor or AngiesList have aggressive marketing campaigns and can provide you with leads you would not otherwise receive. The key is to respond quickly to these leads before another contractor snatches up the customer.

Gig work:

If you are a freelancer, you likely spend 20-30% of your time every week looking for the next gig. Online directories can help with freelancers as well. Freelancer.com and UpWork.com both connect freelancers with gigs. Some of these can come from national, unexpected sources.

Don't discount the phone book:

You might remember back to the pre-internet days of thumbing through the yellow pages to find the number for the local pizza delivery service. Whereas the printed phone book is typically only used by older shoppers, their online directory service can prove to be helpful. A service like DexKnows.com or YellowPages.com can provide your business with increased connectivity throughout the web and higher-ranking internet search results.

Section 2: Creating a Website That Sells

The Basics of a Lead-Generating Website

Now that you've established who you are trying to sell to and what drives them to take action, it's time to start putting together a website that motivates your audience to purchase your products or services.

A website is more than words and pictures on a page. How those words are written and laid-out will either motivate the visitor to take action or not. The main purpose of a small-business website is to attract new leads and to make sales, so let's start out with the basics of online lead generation.

A Lead-Generating Website Strategy

You need a way to stand out online. There are likely other companies who do what you do and both your business and theirs can be found online. So how do you stand out? How do you get the job?

People can find a lot of information these days on the internet. As a result, the traditional method of simply explaining your services doesn't engage with buyers as effectively as it used to. Simply put, you can't just put a laundry list of your services or a description of your product's merits on the internet and expect people to call. **Information alone on a website does not generate leads.**

The key to a lead-generation strategy is to build trust. You want your business to be at the top-of-mind for shoppers when they are ready to make purchases. This top-of-mind awareness is not gained primarily by your logo showing up on internet advertisements. *Status as an expert has to be earned.*

Once a visitor hits your site, it needs to be apparent that you are an expert at what you do. This perceived expertise comes from great content, excellent reviews, and good photography. Additionally, it can come through a digital resource like an eBook, a compelling infographic, or downloadable guide. You can start generating great leads from your website when you stop trying to be a pesky salesperson and instead start showing that you really know what you're doing and that you genuinely care about your customer's experience. Making this switch helps to convert you from being the cold-calling sales person to the trusted expert whom others are calling for advice.

So, how do you make this happen?

Four tips to become a market expert on your website and capture leads:

1. **Understand the problem**. Your potential customers are coming to you to help them solve a problem. They might need their plumbing fixed.

They might need a new car. Either way, there is a pain point. They have a problem that they need you to solve for them. Understanding this problem and providing content on the web to address their issue will help you to be seen as a friend and a trusted expert.

2. **Give away some resources.** Once you figure out the problem your customers are coming to you to solve, then give away a resource that will help them better understand the solution to their problem. For example, a potential customer might come to a flooring contractor because their floors are worn out. By offering a guide to new, modern flooring options and styles, the contractor could help them get excited about not only getting new flooring, but updating the whole look of their house. Try to provide added value by helping your customers learn about something they are already interested in purchasing.

3. **Promote the resource you're giving away.** Write some posts on your social media pages or take out an ad on Facebook that offers the resource for free. Rather than designing an ad with just a logo on it, the flooring contractor could promote the "Free Guide to Modern Flooring." Potential customers are far more likely to engage with that type of advertisement.

4. **Collect information in exchange for the resource.** So, you're not really giving it away for free. Someone is paying for the resource by trading it for their contact information. Once you have their contact information, you can retarget them for upcoming sales, special offers and limited-time coupons. People are happy to offer email addresses for something of value to them. Once you have their email address, your email engine can then take over and continue marketing for you while your focus is on other aspects of your business.

A good lead-generation website strategy is an effective way to establish yourself as an expert and to attract better clientele.

Guiding Real People Through Your Website

A potential customer came to your website because they have a real problem to solve. Now that they are on your site, you need to become a website guide and provide a real, trustworthy solution to their problem. When they visit your site, you are guiding them on a path of discovery so that you can prove to that person, one step at a time, that using your product or service will make their life easier and will provide the experience they were looking to find.

Sure, asking them to make a purchase outright is easier to do and takes less effort, but getting creative and offering superb content will help your customers not just be nameless, digital consumers. Rather, they will become brand ambassadors.

So, become a storyteller, be a website guide, and take your customers on a journey! Here are a few steps for getting that done:

Not Digital People, But Real People in a Digital Environment

Your audience is not data on a chart. To sell your product or services effectively, you need to make human connections with your customers. You need to know what they want so you can tailor a service or product to fit their needs.

Previously, we talked about creating a persona for your target audience. I mentioned a business who identified their customer and even put a picture of her up so that the promotional team would not forget who she was. **If you don't market to a target audience, you'll usually end up marketing to yourself!**

By creating an audience persona, you gain a better understanding of what is motivating people to visit your website. When you understand why they are there, then you'll also better understand why they make purchases.

If your target audience is a 44-year-old woman, don't just think about her. Think about what she likes, what she drives, what she does for fun, who her friends are, what her family is like, what she listens to on the radio, what makes her sad, what challenges she faces, and what her hobbies might be.

Once you understand who your customer is and what your customer is looking for, a good website guide brings a customer through the buying process. Here is a description of the buying process. It is often referred to as a "sales funnel":

Typical Sales Funnel

A consumer will move through a process with your company in these stages before they make a purchase: Awareness, Consideration, and Conversion.

Let's briefly unpack those three stages:

Awareness:

You may be offering the very best service in town, but that doesn't do anyone any good if they don't know that you exist. Awareness got them to your website in the first place. A lot of marketing is involved in this stage. Print and digital pieces that can help with awareness include:

- Signs, banners / flags, storefront graphics, vehicle graphics
- Direct and EDDM mail, print ads, business cards, flyers
- Digital ads, social media ads
- Radio / broadcast

However, once the customer is on your site, you are out of the awareness stage. So, don't redouble your awareness efforts here. Your website is all about the process of consideration. As a website guide, you are not helping the user discover your company. You are helping them decide if they are going to trust you or not.

Consideration:

Once people hear about you, they begin to investigate what it is that you do. This is the reason they are on your website. Now it's the time to show that you really know your stuff! As a website guide, you can help a customer make up their mind by using:

- Blog posts
- Testimonials
- Photography
- Videos
- Webinars

Conversion:

Ultimately, your goal is to make a conversion. You are trying to move a lead through the process of turning them into a paying customer and ultimately into an advocate for your company.

A Website Guide Leads Users Through the Sales Funnel

Walk the customer through the process in this sales funnel. Set goals for them along the way. For example, when they get to the front page, what should be their first step of discovery? Create a link and a button to get them there. If they read a blog post, what should they read next? Create a link and a path for a user to take through your site that leads them from one content page to the next.

Then, along the way, make it clear what their next sales step might be. Do you want them to buy from your store? Do you want them to schedule a consultation? Make sure there are clear directions and clear navigation links to get them from one step to the next.

Not Just a Digital Transaction, but a Real Relationship

The user's visit to your website is not just data and a transaction. It is an opportunity for you to tell the story of your business and guide your customer on a journey to discover more about what interests them. As you become a trusted guide, you'll build a deeper relationship with your client and you'll find them coming back to you over and over again.

Four Essentials for Small Business Websites

If you are a small business owner, a potential customer may only give your site a few seconds before they move on to your competitor's. **If your site is simple, clear, functional, and professional, it will generate more business.**

Simple is better. So, let me ask you 3 questions to determine if your website is simple enough:

- Can a new user easily determine <u>what you do</u> by looking at your website for **5 seconds**?

- If they are looking for a product that you sell, could they simply and easily <u>find out information</u> about that product from your site in **10 seconds**?

- Do they understand from your site the simple factors that separate you from others in your area offering similar services?

Your website needs to communicate to potential customers what *you* do in language they can clearly comprehend. If you aren't seeing traffic come in for your website, **here are a few tips** that might help you to attract more business from the web:

#1: Make the Home Page Simple, Clear and Responsive

Google is by far the most widely used search engine and part of their success comes from keeping it simple. Research has found that people can process fewer than 10 different options on a webpage, so Google keeps their homepage choices extremely limited. Being an effective website guide means that you don't give people too many choices to make. You always help users know exactly how to take the next step.

Things that look simple are often the result of a great deal of planning. Map out your site before you begin. Consider placing no more than 6–7 choices on the home page and then make those choices really clear! Think about how a person travels through your site and ask:

- What are they going to see first? What impression does that image make?

- Where do you want the customer to go next? What do you want each step to communicate about your company?

- What can you offer on the website that will turn a person from a browser to a buyer?

Consider interviewing some regular customers and ask them what convinced them to use your products and/or services over those of your competitors. Use this input to help move a website viewer through your site so they become your next regular customer.

#2: Remove Unnecessary Clutter

Over time, websites tend to get cluttered up. Managers begin to push for more space to promote products, salespeople promise clients space on the website, new products are being offered by the production team, and negotiations are made with new vendors. New blogs get added. Content evolves. Before long, your site can become a mess!

Begin by **shortening long lists** of services and condense them into simple-to-understand statements. Better yet, tell stories and highlight experiences. People aren't as interested in a laundry list of your services as they are with knowing that you are an expert and working with you will be a pleasurable experience. Put the main ideas into titles and headers. You have less than 10 seconds to communicate to a new buyer what you do, so <u>make sure your main message stands out!</u>

Secondly, **use stock photos intelligently**. A stock photo is better than no photo, but our last update from Google informed us that the engine is ranking sites higher that utilize real images and custom photography. Stock images can be effective communication tools, but they need to be carefully chosen to reinforce the message of the text. When possible, use professionally shot images of your staff and your products. <u>Realism goes a long way when promoting a small business.</u>

Thirdly, **use terminology that those outside of your industry can understand**. Technical jargon can be helpful in the shop, but it can be confusing to the general public. Consider having someone outside your company read your promotional copy before you publish it. <u>Make sure that someone who is unfamiliar with your product understands what you are offering.</u>

#3: Connect to Social Media

Social media marketing is exploding! **Small businesses who utilize social media are attracting new customers**. Include "like" and "share" features on your website. Give people an opportunity to interact with what they see there.

Produce new content on your site on a regular basis. Twice a month is a minimum. Once a week is better! Sites that add new content 10–15 times per month are currently getting the best results. Write about what you know and then share it on both your website and your social media pages. Give your customers the chance to share that information with others. Give people a reason to keep coming back to your site by offering up new content.

People trust those who are experts in their field. You have the opportunity to use your site to position yourself as an expert in your area. Your main objective is to earn the trust of your customers with your web content.

#4: We are No Longer "Above the Fold"—JUST LET THEM SCROLL!

Ten years ago, the conventional wisdom was to keep all critical information about the company on the very first screenshot, before the user has to scroll. This idea is so outdated.

People scroll. They *WANT to* Scroll. **JUST LET THEM SCROLL!** Most modern websites use 3–5 clearly marked sections to draw the reader through the content on the home page. These sections should include a few (but not all) of these elements:

1. **A value proposition** is a photo-reinforced tagline. These are often called "sliders" by web programmers. This element is a one-line statement that tells a user everything they need to know about who you are. It is the first visual impression.

2. **An intro video** showing the owners, your product, or your services. Everything has an orientation video these days and they are very effective!

3. **A graphic overview of services**. Don't just list them all. Guide the reader through your main products or services using icons or images.

4. **Testimonials** really help to build trust—especially if you are relatively new or unknown.

5. The "**About Us**" section of every website I've ever built is one of the most visited features. People who visit small businesses want to know who they are dealing with.

6. Feature *a few* of your most **popular products.**

7. **Case Studies / Work Samples / Success Stories** all help to build trust with a potential client.

8. People will come back repeatedly if you offer some helpful resources. **Resources** often come in the form of a blog or news page.

One huge exception to the "let them scroll" rule is search engines and logins. Both logins and search engines should generally still be "above the fold."

For just about everything else, we are not trying to cram everything together at the top anymore, so <u>use white space</u>. Don't cram it all in...let the page breathe. Be more liberal with pictures and use your headings intentionally.

Wix vs. Weebly vs. WordPress: Why We Suggest WordPress to Build Websites

What Are the Most Popular Options for Building Websites?

The three major platforms for designing and creating websites are Wix, Weebly, and WordPress. Each choice possesses some appealing features. However, if you decide to have a professionally-constructed site, and you should, **WordPress is hands-down the best option for most small businesses**.

Wix Versus WordPress

In recent years, Wix has skyrocketed in popularity. Many celebrities and high-profile people are hosted on Wix. However, WordPress remains the preferred establishment for about a third of internet promotion for businesses. While both Wix and WordPress are fine platforms, they are quite different in many respects. Here is the most important distinction:

- **Wix is a site builder.** That means it is user-friendly and most technical issues will be resolved for you.

- **WordPress is a powerful content management system** (CMS) which allows the user to add, edit, and remove content from a website without involving a webmaster. However, WordPress requires more technical knowledge.

So, the bottom line is that you can make changes to your content faster and more efficiently with WordPress, but you need to have a little bit of technical know-how or the time to research. WordPress is fairly intuitive, but the learning curve can be a little steep for first-time users.

Weebly Versus WordPress

Weebly is also something of a rising star, with over 50 million sites. Yet WordPress still dominates the field. Like Wix, Weebly is significantly different than WordPress:

- **Wix is an all-in-one builder.** It is good for beginners but has some limitations in the way you can design it. For non-coders, it can be an acceptable option.

- **WordPress is a self-hosted open-source platform.** That means that you can create a site completely from scratch. Wix has everything built in for you, making it easy to construct a website. However, you will wind up with more of a "cookie-cutter" type of online promotion than is possible with WordPress.

Again, if a company of professional experts designs your website, there is no limit to your creativity, flair, and branding. Your effectiveness in online marketing will be outstanding!

Why is WordPress the Best Choice?

Wordpress provides a small-business web designer with the power to create the best, unique, custom-designed websites for nearly any kind of business. It offers speed, mobile responsiveness, and built-in SEO abilities. The adaptability, beauty, and functionality of a WordPress site is currently unmatched on other platforms.

9 Essential WordPress Tips

As we've established, WordPress is by far the best and most adaptive website builder. Our team works with WordPress websites every day. Here are a few tips for getting the most out of yours:

1. Be familiar with the dashboard!

- The dashboard is the main screen you land at after logging in. Spend a few minutes learning how things are organized in WordPress.

- The main menu sidebar is on the left—this sidebar is where you navigate to create posts and pages, customize your website's appearance, access settings, etc.

- At the very top, you'll see your website's name and a few quickly-accessible links. Clicking on your website name opens the front-end of your site.

2. Distinguish posts content from pages content:

- **Posts** work great for blog content. Posts are designed to be easily shareable, searchable, and comment-able. You can schedule them to be published at future dates and times, and you can choose to make them appear on your site in any order desired. Posts are meant to be added often and updated frequently.

- **Pages** work great for content that won't change much over time, like your "About" page or "Contact" page. Pages are displayed in your top navigation bar and menus. It's important not to use pages for information like news, events, recaps, updates, reviews, or opinions that are better contained within posts.

3. Focus on your titles:

Your post and page titles are what help your audience make a quick decision about whether to click on your content or not. Titles are also important because Google indexes them for search results. Create titles that are:

- **Engaging:** Grab their attention.

- **Insightful:** Let your audience know what they'll learn and what they'll gain.

- **Clear:** Quickly inform your viewers what the topic is. Use appropriate search terms, but don't repeat the same keywords over and over.

4. Don't plagiarize:

It is actually against the law to use copyrighted media without permission from the owner. Also, Google is looking for sites with original content. Only add content to your site that fits into one of these categories:

- You made it yourself
- You asked for the original owner's permission
- It is already available for anyone to use under the public domain

5. Optimize your photos:

- **Compress:** The photos you upload to your website should be sized under 1MB—this smaller file size helps your site run faster and allows for more overall storage space. Yes, it's an extra step, but it doesn't take long. Kraken.io, ResizeImage, and Optimizilla are a few free online tools you can use to optimize your image.
- **Resize:** After you upload an image to WordPress, you can edit the image and resize it to fit whatever your page or post needs. WordPress lets you flip images, mirror them, and scale and crop.

6. Keep your sidebar simple:

It's easy to cram a ton of widgets into your sidebar, but if you use too many, they can take away from the content you really want your visitors to engage with.

Assess your sidebar, and if your sidebar becomes overloaded, edit it down. Ruthlessly. Experiment and see how simplifying it affects your site's traffic.

7. Avoid installing too many plugins:

Yes, there are a lot of great plugins out there, but that doesn't mean you need them all. Installing too many plugins, or low-quality plugins, can affect the speed of your website. Reliable plugins are compatible with WordPress's latest version and will have good reviews, support forums, and frequent updates. The first plugin to consider when getting started is for SEO. The most popular one is called "Yoast"—it makes sure you're following good Google search index guidelines, like keyword density and meta descriptions.

You might also want to consider a security plugin. Make sure to add plugins one at a time to make sure they work properly with the rest of your site and always deactivate and uninstall the ones you decide to stop using.

8. Update to avoid site crashes:

If you don't continually update WordPress and your theme, your site becomes vulnerable to security attacks. If you don't update your plugins, they can actually make your site crash. Turn on automatic updates or check every few days and update them manually.

9. Run backups of your site!

Backups are extremely important. There are hackers out there who would love to steal your data, but there are also user errors that you might make. The best way to make sure you're consistently backing up your site is to automate it with a plugin. "Jetpack" offers many different helpful features: daily backups, a contact form, a mobile theme, security, and faster image loading.

3 Proven Ways to Drive Website Sales

Consumers on the internet make some really fast decisions. People will usually decide whether they are going to learn more about your product in eight seconds or less, so those first eight seconds need to be pretty stellar!

Keep in mind that while they are looking at your product or company, they are probably looking at your competitors as well. Potential customers will be trying to make an educated decision about whether to call you or to call the other guy.

So, from a marketing standpoint, I want to give you three quick suggestions for helping your website make more conversions. Those are: Mobile Responsiveness, Photography, and Free Offers.

#1: Mobile Speed and Responsiveness Help Drive Website Sales

Unless you're a caveman, you've probably realized by now that more than half of your internet traffic is coming from mobile devices. But having your website just "work" on a mobile device is not good enough these days. In today's digital marketplace, your website needs to work well and be optimized for mobile viewing.

Mobile-friendliness is a big part of Google's current algorithm:

What this means is that Google will give ranking preference to websites that display content properly and quickly on mobile devices. If your site does not work well on mobile, then you can expect it to drop in the rankings and a decrease in your online sales conversions.

Speeding up your site on mobile often means that you need to:

- Load pictures in at a smaller size
- Reduce the number of slides in a slider
- Turn off various features that load well on a desktop but that don't translate well to a mobile device
- Uninstall apps that are outdated, malfunctioning, or unused
- Remove all the themes from your website besides the one you are using and the latest theme from WordPress

There are a variety of WordPress templates that respond quickly and effectively to various screen sizes and shapes. This type of responsiveness is critical for website conversions.

#2: Proper Photography Helps to Drive Website Sales

You could have a silent enemy lurking around your beautifully designed website, threatening to overthrow and devour your online presence. That enemy is stock photography!

Does that sound a little overdramatic? Well, maybe it is, but both the user's experience and Google's algorithm can be negatively affected by totally fake pictures.

Both the algorithm and your users are looking for quality and authenticity. On the other hand, a stock representation of your services or products is better than just text.

Use authentic pictures:

All studies show that pictures do help with conversions. We use stock images all the time and they have their place, but stock pictures that are not really carefully chosen can come across as fake.

If you are given a choice between a fake photo with perfect-looking people in it or a high-quality photo with your actual staff, choose the real picture every time!

Also, front-facing people make a good first impression that work trucks and machinery don't. Make sure that the top image on your site is welcoming.

#3: Free Offers Help to Drive Website Sales

Okay, so who doesn't like free stuff?

Most websites that convert have a free offer or a coupon on their homepage or another of the main pages. You can offer free things like:

- Free eBook
- Free shipping
- Free subscription
- Free newsletter
- Free consultation
- Free estimate

Free offers are incredibly effective for increasing your conversions!

There is a lot that could be helpful when thinking about your website, but for now make sure your site works as well on a mobile device as it does on a desktop, take the time and spend the money to get real, high-quality photos, and make a great offer that is free if possible.

Three Tactics for Keeping Potential Buyers on Your Website Longer

If you want to keep visitors on your website, you'll discover that it's a bit of a balancing act. You want to present information that is dynamic and engaging. You also don't want to overdo it so that your site seems overwhelming or cluttered. In this article, we are going to discuss what is often referred to as "user flow."

You don't want visitors to lose interest until they schedule an appointment or purchase a product. You want to make every effort to guide a customer on such a compelling journey through your site so that they want to spend more time taking in all you have to offer.

Have you ever been to a restaurant that offered a few too many good things to choose from on their menu? Too many good options all at once can make it nearly impossible to decide! When I visit a restaurant, I want to have enough good choices to keep my interest, but not so many that I suffer from paralysis by analysis. Your website should follow the same principle. If you give people too many options all at one time, they will feel overwhelmed and click away. Give them just a few options at a time and guide them through the journey.

The answer isn't less content. In fact, some studies are showing that you need to add at least 2 posts per month on your blog and the best results often are found between 10–16 posts per month. That's a lot of content! However, without a good "user flow," a visitor can easily get lost.

So, here are three tweaks you can make to your site to help organize your pages and create a good "user flow":

3 Keys for Good User Flow

Tap into the psychology of internet browsing:

The psychology here is simpler than it seems. Take a minute to think about why a user might stop and read a page. Something drew them there and a clean layout will help keep them there.

Simply put, write interesting headlines that help draw a reader's eye down the page and that re-engages them as they read. A site with good user flow continually draws the reader from one section to the next.

Use front-facing pictures that feature interesting people. For example, a smiling electrician at work is more engaging than a picture of the electrician's truck. Make the site uncluttered and easy to read.

Then, use social proof to your advantage. Testimonies of satisfied customers are really compelling. Add testimonies onto your pages and posts. Happy customers help to inspire trust in those who are coming to you for the first time.

Drive action forward:

Keep people clicking. You can't get someone to click to buy a product or to schedule an appointment until you get them clicking on your site.

Always give your user the next step you want them to take. Don't lead them to a dead end. Good user flow means that every page should lead to the next. Keep your visitors engaged by giving them a teaser for another article on every page.

Website readers enjoy reading posts that are simple and easy to understand. When you offer a next step to take, make sure it's not confusing to the reader where they should go next. If you use a button to lead them to the next step, some studies are now suggesting that red buttons attract more clicks than, say, green buttons do.

Use widgets effectively:

WordPress offers a huge array of widgets that help with everything from navigation to embedding YouTube videos and posting advertisements. Utilizing widgets, you can make useful footers, you update areas throughout the site, or promote the latest article site-wide with just a few clicks.

Learn User Flow As You Go

At the end of the day, if you only see users visiting one or two pages, don't panic. That is normal. You can start to battle those trends through excellent content, excellent navigation, eye-catching layout and good user flow.

When Is It Time to Call a Web Designer?

Did you know that it takes less than one tenth of a second for a person to form an opinion about your business from the appearance of your website? The previous article mentioned that after that initial impression is made, a user will need to find what they are looking for in eight seconds or less or they will likely click away.

Many businesses think that building their own website is a good and cost-effective way to go. Unless you have an experienced web designer on your staff, you might consider outsourcing your site to someone who makes websites for a living. Your website is one of your most important marketing assets and dedicating some time and money to your site can have a huge impact on your success.

Here are some ways a well-designed site can help your business:

- **Stay ahead of your competition:** You want to be on the cutting edge in your field, and you want potential customers to know it! A professional design will give you an important advantage over your competitors.

- **Increase consumer engagement:** Professionalism in design and content keeps website visitors glued to the promotion of your business. Continued customer engagement leads to purchases!

- **Keywords get you to the top of the page**: An excellent internet marketing firm will research keywords and know how and where to use them. The right words and phrases will bring you high rankings on the search engines.

- **Well-structured content is essential:** Many businesses are so focused on the tiny details of their content, they tend to overlook the importance of structure, content, and alignment that make pages easy to view and user-friendly. Organization and eye-catching graphics are as critical as keywords and phrases.

- **Express your brand image:** The brand image that your prospects view online has a lot of impact in influencing their loyalty towards your company.

- **DIY internet marketing often lacks eye-appeal:** A site professionally designed by an artist is far more exceptional in visual appeal than "do-it-yourself" design attempts.

Some DIY websites are remarkably good and I hope this guide will be a huge asset to you if you are trying to do it yourself. However, if you come to a place where you just can't get it to work, or it just doesn't make any sense to you, then it might be time to hire a great web designer to help you out.

Section 3: Effectively Using Print Media to Promote Your Website

Creating an Effective Low-Tech Direct Mail Campaign to Drive Website Traffic

At the beginning of this booklet, we mentioned that recent studies have shown that there is a basic foundation every business needs to establish before they start getting too fancy, creative or complicated with their marketing strategy.

You could picture the marketing strategy for most small businesses as a train. The train engine that fuels the most basic functions of your marketing efforts is threefold:

1. Your website
2. Your email drip systems, and
3. Your printed advertisements.

Without these basic three in place, most businesses find that other media types are less effective. (Not that they are not effective, just that they are less effective.)

Once print, web, and email are in place, then you can fuel your efforts though content marketing. As content is added and you come to be seen as an expert, then social media, podcasts, newspaper columns, and broadcasts become a lot more effective.

In this next section, I want to focus on the print aspect of your marketing engine.

Every Business Requires Continual Visibility with Potential Customers

Big businesses have the budgets to buy huge spreads in national, glossy magazines. That probably is not you, so let's recap a few principles about small business marketing we previously shared:

- Smaller businesses with residential services often have good luck in local neighborhood magazines.
- If your product costs less than $100, then a coupon mailer could be effective.

Still, these options can be more expensive than a really small business can afford. *(Like the kind of business that is just a husband and wife team with a truck and some tools.)* So, if you are just getting started, let me talk a little bit about high-touch, low-tech postcard marketing. Postcards can be a really simple and effective way of driving traffic to your website. Once they are on your website, then you can go into greater detail about your expertise and your unique services.

There are a few reasons why you still get glossy postcards and greeting cards in the mail during this digital age:

1. **Postcards are impossible to avoid.** They make an impression as soon as people see them. Even if they go right in the trash, they make that impression the entire way to the trash can. A well-designed piece on thick, glossy paper can feel really valuable and will often sit on a desk or countertop for a long period of time, making impressions the entire time it is there.

2. **Glossy postcards help your business to look serious and established.** Digital marketing is also really effective, but it can also feel temporary and impersonal. Postcards appear to take more labor and effort to deliver, so people will often take them more seriously.

3. **Postcards are extremely targeted.**

4. You can send a mailer to just your former customer list and, in doing so, you know that you're marketing to red-hot clients.

5. Some greeting card services will allow you to automatically send cards to people on their birthday and other significant occasions.

6. You can target a neighborhood through Every Door Direct Mail (EDDM) and know that everyone in that key neighborhood is going to see your piece.

7. You can acquire a list through the Chamber or a lead service that is put together for your demographic.

8. In all these cases, postcards are very specific in their target.

Best Practices for Cost-Effective Postcard Promotion

Glossy, color postcards are relatively inexpensive to produce and deliver. Research has shown that direct mail is most effective when you follow these guidelines:

1. **Use a headline that is 7 words or less.** Tell them the rest of your story on your website.

2. **Use a single, eye-catching photo or just a couple well-chosen pictures.** Less is more! Front facing, smiling women are always a safe bet. White space (or empty space) is your friend and will help with readability. Avoid putting on long laundry lists of services. Put on a featured service that is a good entry point into your business. A customer will find out more of what you do as they get to know you.

3. **Use a minimal amount of text and make a call to action very clear.** People need to know what you are offering or what you're asking them to do when they get the mailer.

4. **Make it client-focused.** Show and describe the user experience rather than talking about your company.

5. **Use high-quality paper.** People are less likely to throw away a postcard advertisement that feels substantial

Using these techniques will help your business stand out and grab your customers' attention while not breaking the bank.

Using Magazine Ads to Drive Traffic to Your Website

Have you ever been to a party and sat next to someone who spends the whole time talking about themselves? It gets old really fast and (if you're like me) you try to find the exit as soon as possible.

What if I told you that many small businesses make this same social mistake with their magazine ads?

Instead of speaking to the needs of a potential client, too many small business ads are focused more on letting people know how fantastic they are with a huge logo and laundry list of services. They brag about their services as if they are trying to bore people into buying.

Guess what…that approach doesn't usually work very well.

So much of what I see is the equivalent of watching an advertising car crash. It's like paragraphs of words were on a collision course with each other and spilled out all over the page.

Instead, Highlight One Product and Direct People to Your Website

On your website, you can take buyers through a compelling journey and spend time with them explaining your products and services.

Common Print Advertising Mistakes

I've been designing ads for a couple of decades. Let me share the thought process behind many small business ad layouts. The owner or manager calls me and says:

- "We want you to make us an ad. So…start with a huge version of our logo in the corner….No, no, no, make it big….Ummm….Still bigger…"
- "Now, in a 6 point font, list out these 25 services that our company does."
- "Then add our tagline: 'The Best in Northern Arizona.'"
- "Okay, now put our truck on there…we love that thing. And a picture of the owner—he loves to see himself."
- "Make sure to put on our phone number really big and no one will be able to resist our huge offer of a free quote."

Instead of using their advertising assets together, they try to make each advertising piece tell the entire story of their business every time.

These businesses are hoping that on the very day that a potential customer opens up the magazine, they'll read an ad all about the business owner, see their huge logo, services in a tiny font, a picture of the owner or their truck and think: "Man I've got to talk to this guy some more. I can't wait to hear them talk about themselves...I wonder if there is a free consultation."

You could call this approach "marketing by ego," but it's far from effective. The owner is hoping someone will hear them talking about themselves at the magazine advertising party and want to hear more.

Here's the rub, it works sometimes...

Sometimes, by bragging, a business will pull someone away from the crowd at the party and make a sale. Then the owner is usually left wondering why that approach doesn't work all the time and, in the end, they often spend more money on these laundry-list, self-promoting ads than they make in sales at the end of the month.

They don't want to miss the occasional drip and dribble of business that results from the ads. However, if you can't track $3-4 of profit for every $1 you spend on advertising, then either your advertising or your tracking isn't working properly.

Questions to Ask Before Designing Your Next Print Ad

Before you take out your next ad, you need to ask two vital questions:

1. What is the single purpose of your ad?
2. What one thing does your ad focus on?

Nine times out of ten, the purpose should be to highlight one product and then to direct people to your website.

When most small business owners are asked about their objectives for any given advertisement, they usually spout out a list like this: The ad is for...

- Branding,
- Getting my name out there,
- Letting people know about all my services,
- Making sales, and
- Getting people to call in for a quote.

In the meantime, your audience is getting bored and you've lost the sale. First let's start with a misconception about branding.

A Misconception About Branding

First of all, huge companies have huge budgets and they can afford to spend untold thousands of dollars on branding campaigns. Most small businesses can't fathom a marketing budget of this magnitude, so they just can't market themselves like they are Nike, Coke, or even the local hospital.

When I talk about branding, I mean the strategy of placing your logo all over the place with no additional compelling content and expecting that to pass for advertising.

A logo-driven, branding-only strategy will bankrupt many small businesses. Most need to stop focusing primarily on branding and start focusing primarily on positioning themselves as experts. The best place to talk to your customers and to establish yourself as a trusted voice is on your website!

But, instead of driving potential customers to an informative, professional website, many small business owners try to make the most out of every square inch of tiny ad in an attempt to get the biggest bang for their buck. **By trying to do it all, every time, in every ad, they accomplish none of it and completely waste their money. They lose the sale.**

How to Use Print Advertising Effectively

Here are a few rules of thumb:

1. Highlight one thing at a time.
2. Have a clear call to action. Typically, it will be to visit your website.
3. Take down every distraction from your message in the ad (even if that distraction is your logo, a picture of your owner, and a picture of your truck).

Unfortunately, you are in a crowded market. If everyone is shouting "LOOK AT ME!" with their huge logo and laundry lists of services, then it all just becomes background noise.

By contrast, an ad that focuses on solving a single problem in a memorable and compelling fashion will stand out from 99% of the other advertisements in the same publication.

Section 4: Email Marketing

Your Email Sales Machine

Do you want to convert more of your sales leads automatically? What if you could hire an extra set of hands to warm up cold leads and even close a sale before you pick up the phone? What if you could create an automated sales machine? It sounds like a dream, right?

Now, no marketing tool is a magic bullet, but an effective email campaign might be the closest thing to it. And, it is one of the least-expensive tools in the small business marketing arsenal.

Email Autoresponders Are One of the Most Effective Marketing Tools

Once again, I'll reiterate that all research shows the top three most effective marketing pieces for a small business are a good website, at least one regular targeted print advertisement (postcards, newspaper, magazines, etc.), and an effective email strategy. Without these three in place, the effectiveness of other techniques is considerably less.

In this section, I want to talk about creating an effective email autoresponder series. Email autoresponders can be used to retarget existing customers or to cross-sell products, but here I'm going to focus on autoresponders that warm up new leads. There are many online tools out there right now like Mail Chimp, Constant Contact, and aWeber that offer a user-friendly way to program email autoresponders yourself.

First of all, let's cover what an email responder is.

What Is an Email Autoresponder?

An email autoresponder is a pre-programmed series of emails that are sent to a segmented part of your contact list. These emails are typically triggered by a specific event such as:

- Signing up for regular email updates or news from a form on your website

- Abandoning a shopping cart (if you have an ecommerce site)

- Adding a contact manually to a list after getting a business card at a networking event

- Signing up for a free download, like an ebook from a landing page or internet advertisement

I was recently doing some market research for a client who installs flooring and I came across an opportunity to download a "Look Book" from his competitor. As a marketer, I wanted to see what my client's competitor had created, so I signed up. I entered my email address and, in my inbox came this beautifully designed eBook that featured applications for various types of flooring.

This technique is what marketers often call a lead magnet. There is an appealing offer for something you want and an exchange made online. "I'll give you my personal information if you give me access to a free download, a product, or a service."

Once you have this lead, you can begin to use your autoresponder to nurture it.

Email Autoresponders Nurture New Leads

Naturally, I'm skeptical about companies I meet online, so it could take me some time to get to know them. Email autoresponders begin to take an icy, unfamiliar client and turn them into someone who sees you as familiar and trustworthy.

Your pre-programmed email drip campaign puts your name in their inbox on a regular basis and, as you are able to draw them in with interesting subject lines and great content, you build up your business as the expert in your area.

In other words, autoresponders build relationships and credibility with new leads from the moment they join your list. Then, they create an automatic onboarding process to assist your sales team.

Email Autoresponders Turn Leads Into Customers

Ultimately, your goal is to make an impression so you can convert cold leads into paying customers. A well-programmed email series will help a new lead get to know your business.

Then, as you continue to share your quality work, they will begin to like your business.

Finally, as you consistently prove that you are the leading expert, customers begin to trust your business.

A sales phone call with a customer who already knows, likes and trusts you, is pre-programmed for success from the start.

First Impressions Matter:
Great Email Subject Lines Draw in Readers

First impressions matter. That's true in person and it's true online. It's also true with email. The subject line of your email is the very first thing a reader sees and is often the determining factor in whether or not they will open that email from you.

Email subject lines can drive the next move for a consumer. Either they will be curious and open it, or they will dump it in the trash.

Email marketing is the absolute best for the dollar spent, but you can decimate a subscriber list if you inundate them with emails that are of no interest to them. Mastering the art of email subject lines is essential to your success as an email marketer.

Email Subject Lines by the Stats

When you write a really compelling email subject line, it can lead to a higher open rate for your emails. If more of your emails are opened, then that has a direct correlation to your online sales. It also fosters a sense of community amongst your followers. Developing yourself as an expert should be your main objective online. A great email marketing campaign can be a huge asset in that quest.

Several studies have been done on email subject lines. Here are three principles they found:

1. **Keep your subject line clear and concise.** Subject lines with 61-70 characters have the highest open rates. That roughly translates to 10 words or less.

2. **Short subject lines fit better on a mobile screen.** More than half of all email is now viewed on mobile devices. Subject lines that are cut off by a mobile device screen may prove to be less effective

3. **Personalization is helpful.** Placing the name of your contact in the subject line can increase your open rate by as much as 18%.

Engage with Your Audience

Studies have found that 33% of emails are opened based on the subject line alone. Good email subject lines will engage your reader and draw them in to read about something they care about. Here are some strategies you can experiment with:

1. **A personal connection with your reader.** Think less about what you want to email to accomplish and more about communicating with your reader. I have had great success with short emails that simply read something like this: "Hey, <fname>, I thought I would touch base with you today to see if there is anything you need from us. We love working with you and we'd like to continue to earn your business. Please email me back and let me know how we can serve you better. Mark."

2. **Tap into emotions.** Emotions are great motivators. Appeal to your readers' curiosity or excitement. Send out a funny story or picture. Make it so your readers look forward to the interesting content inside your email and can't wait to open them up.

3. **Make it urgent.** There is nothing more compelling than a limited time, special offer. Something like a one-day sale can motivate a reader to make an immediate decision instead of putting it off until later.

4. **Create a cliffhanger.** You'll get more clicks if you pique the curiosity of those receiving your emails.

5. **Be exciting.** Talk about big news or exciting updates. Use strong words and language to bring a ray of levity and happiness to your customer's day.

A Final Thought

Speak in your company's voice. Every business and brand has a certain personality. Don't be playful and ultra-positive one day, then serious and ultra-academic the next. Understand the voice of your business and speak to your audience in a consistent way.

75 Effective Email Subject Lines

There was a recent study done of 100 effective email subject lines. I've included some examples that I think will inspire you as you put together your email marketing campaigns. Here are the reasons behind why they were found to be effective:

Self-Interest

In broadcasting, we often said that everyone's favorite station is W.I.I.F.M.— What's In It For Me.

WIIFM subject lines are your go-to subject lines—you should be using them most frequently. They are usually direct and speak to a specific benefit your audience will gain by opening the email.

Self-interest subject lines also help pre-qualify openers by giving them a clue about your email's body content.

Curiosity

Once in a while, offer a cliffhanger or something that is odd or interesting.

Curiosity-based email lines pique the interest of subscribers without giving away too much information, leading to higher opens.

Be careful, though, because curiosity-based subject lines can get old fast and are the most likely to miss their mark.

Free (or Discounted) Offers

Do you like free stuff? Do you like to buy things?

So do people on your email list.

When you are giving something away or selling something your subscribers would be interested in, directly stating that in your subject line is a great way to convince them to open the email and learn more.

Urgency

One-days sales or announcements of limited supplies are incredible motivators. Subject lines that communicate urgency and scarcity tell readers they must act now. Too many of these can lead to list exhaustion, so use sparingly and, of course, only when there is truly a deadline, limited quantity, or limited availability.

Human Interest

We've seen incredible results from businesses who highlight their local humanitarian outreaches.

Sometimes you need to thank your subscribers for their participation in a local fundraiser, tell them a story about how your business impacted the community, or make a human appeal for their attention.

News

People love knowing the latest news—especially about products and organizations that interest them.

Keeping your audience informed about new developments in your field builds authority and keeps your open rates high. These subject lines often work well when combined with a curiosity element.

Social Proof

Testimonies and satisfied customers help to draw in new customers like magnets. A fundamental characteristic of humans is that we look to the behavior of others when making decisions.

You can leverage this in your email subject lines by mentioning individuals' success stories, familiar names, or highlighting how many people are already using a product or service.

A Great Story

Great stories sell more products than great sales pitches. Telling a story, or at least teasing the beginning of one, in your subject line is a unique way to highlight a benefit and get the open rate you're looking for.

75 Effective Email Subject Lines:

Adapted from content we own from Digital Marketer.

1. (Your Conference) in (an Exotic Location)?
2. Your One-Page Cheat Sheet on _____
3. Sales Up, Refunds Down, Retention Up
4. Your Private Invitation Expires Tomorrow Night
5. Hiring a _____? Here Is Your Guide
6. Let's Fix You Your Offer Together
7. _____ + _____ Tech Stack
8. I Have Some Good News and Some Bad News
9. 4 Critical Questions Your Business Must Answer Right Now
10. I Promise...It's Worth It!
11. Our 7 Best Facebook Ads
12. Start Using This New Facebook Ad Type
13. [Flash Sale] 85% Off Our _____
14. What Happens When You're Approved?
15. Your Content Campaign Planner (Google Doc)
16. [EMAIL TEMPLATE] Fix Your Company's Biggest Marketing Issue
17. (Conference) Day 1 Highlights—News
18. [In Case You Missed It] How to Hire the Right Content Marketer...
19. [LAST CHANCE] 85% Off Sale Ends Today!
20. [CHECKLIST] Get Up to 20% Better Email Deliverability
21. New Facebook Group Features—This Is BIG
22. The Best of (Your Convention)
23. Livestream for (Your Convention) This Year?
24. Tomorrow's the Day...
25. Swipe These 5 Killer Traffic Campaigns
26. The 30-Second Sales Pitch
27. Massive Changes Coming to _____
28. [Infographic] How to Have the Ultimate Experience at _____
29. Is This You?

30. Open Up for Our Best Content

31. Facebook + Pinterest + Video = More Closed Sales

32. You're Invited

33. Paid Traffic Not Converting? Download This...

34. Here's the REAL Reason Amazon is Buying Whole Foods

35. I Knew I Was Right...

36. FINAL NOTICE: "Perfect Offer Mini-Class"

37. _____ Surprised Me with 18 More Sessions

38. Digital Marketing Mastery Is Open!

39. Brand NEW (and Free) Training: 3 Steps to a Perfect Offer

40. How we got 1,329,572 "Earballs" in 20 Months

41. This, Friends, is How You Sell with Email...

42. Class Closes Down Tonight...

43. Important Message (About Tomorrow's Big Announcement)

44. $7 Today, $47 Tomorrow

45. Blog Posts That Sell (A Complete Guide)

46. The Guy Who Made $1,015,209 in One Day...on Amazon

47. Let's Build the Perfect _____ Ad Campaign, Together (for Free)!

48. Claim Your Free _____!

49. The Highest-Level Training We Offer

50. Re: Frequently Asked Question #1

51. [Subscriber] Are You Familiar with _____?

52. Your Perfect Product Launch for $_____

53. Landing Page Not Converting? Try This!

54. Join Me Today at _____ PM

55. Ask Me Anything?

56. [85% Off] 3 Proven _____ Campaigns to Run Today...

57. Join Me in Congratulating...

58. For Advanced Marketers Only!

59. The BIG Shift That's Happening Right Now (and What It Means for You)

60. [POLL] Can You Answer This?

61. [FLASH SALE] My 11-Step Business Launch Plan (and Templates)

62. Finally Monetize Your Email List…

63. Earn Your (Super-Rare) "_____"

64. [Free PDF Download] Claim Our _____ File

65. Does Your _____ Suck? …Or is It "Perfect"?

66. Your (This Year) Business Growth Plan

67. Do NOT Launch Your Product or Service Without This _____

68. [CASE STUDY] 30 Minutes of Work -> _____ Pageviews

69. WIN a Day with _____ & _____ !

70. The Little _____ Tweak That Halved Lead Cost

71. Does Your Ad Type Match Your Offer?

72. Turn Ice-Cold Prospects into Buyers

73. Exciting Announcement (and Special Invitation)

74. How He Built a $20M Ecommerce Brand

75. Facebook Targeting Expansion: The Test (and the Results…)

Section 5: Content Marketing, Social Media, and SEO

Creating Sustainable, Organic Traffic Through Content Marketing

Content marketing refers to the process of writing content related to your company or organization, pushing it out to your blog on a regular basis, programming an SEO plugin to help various search engines index that information, and then cross-promoting it with your social media pages.

For small businesses, this process can bring more and better traffic to your website than nearly any other advertising method. It is a great way to build brand awareness. Better than that, it is a great way to prove that you're an authoritative source for information connected to your \ product or service.

Admittedly, creating content is difficult and can be time-consuming. Content marketing produces long-term traffic rather than immediate traffic. It is always best if the business owner or the leading expert inside the company is the one who develops content. Realistically, the leading expert in your organization is often remarkably busy. Here are a few ideas for developing content from other sources:

- Many small businesses hire an admin to write for them between greeting customers and answering phone calls.
- Other small businesses hire an outside copywriter.
- I know of an engineering firm who hired a college professor to develop content for them.

Developing content isn't impossible, but the organizational leader needs to understand why it is important to accomplish.

Content marketing isn't the engine that drives your marketing. It is more like the coal car. Before you start writing content, you need a well-designed website, a strategy for email marketing, and a regular print advertisement. Content marketing is not a replacement for those marketing assets, but it is the fuel that keeps the engine burning. In this article, I hope to help you understand the place and the importance of content marketing.

Pay-Per-Click Is Good, Organic Search Is Much, Much Better

When you use a search engine, often the first few results are designated as "ads." Those are paid advertisements. Below those paid advertisements are results that the search engine found based on the quality of the content on the pages. Those results are called "organic results."

According to a study in Search Engine Journal, roughly 51% of all web traffic comes from organic searches. Only 10% comes from paid searches. If you want your site to be listed in the 51%, then content marketing is the key!

Creating valuable, high-quality content on your blog, applying SEO tactics, and then cross-promoting those posts on social media all work together to help your content to get found. As a result, your website will come up more frequently in search results.

Here's the bottom line: When you pay to have quality content developed for your site, the content continues to draw in customers for a long time. If you pay for direct advertising, you will only draw customers to your site as long as you continue to pay.

Ad Blockers Are Growing in Popularity

People are increasingly installing software to block annoying paid advertisements, while at the same time they are searching for good content more than ever before.

So, do you want your company operating in the realm of annoying ads or in the realm of excellent content?

In addition to blogs and social media, podcasts and video are becoming increasingly popular mediums. Podcasts and videos allow you to use excellent content to tell stories and entertain your audience.

If I have the choice of which emotion to foster in my audience, I would prefer moving away from annoying them with ads. I would rather inform them with blogs or entertain them with podcasts or videos.

Content Marketing Helps You Build Trust

One of the main purposes of your website should be to establish yourself as a trustworthy expert. Most people will test you out before they buy to see if you really know what you're talking about.

- Free expert advice is excellent salesmanship
- Offer free advice frequently
- Publish free advice often
- Produce podcasts or videos with expert advice and offer those at no charge

When people understand that you are knowledgeable, approachable, and trustworthy, they will gladly pay for your more premium services when the time is right.

Content Marketing Produces the Much-Desired "Word of Mouth" Publicity

When you write an article for your industry that is really helpful or insightful, it tends to get "liked" on social media and shared across the internet. A blog post that attracts a few dozen readers could easily turn into a few sales. A blog post that goes viral across the internet could result in hundreds or thousands of additional sales.

Ads Are Good, Content Marketing Is Simply Better

Pay-per-click ads will drive a little traffic to your website and some businesses find them helpful. However, good content entertains and educates your audience so they know about your brand at a level that is more than logo-deep. It helps your clients to know that you understand their pain points. Content marketing helps to establish you as the authoritative source for your industry.

How Much Is Enough?
Building an Audience by Posting Consistently

When I talk to small businesses about posting consistently, I often get this question: "How much is too much content?" Or, they'll ask me: "How little content can I get away with and still be effective?"

Both are fair questions. If you ask an established blogger or content marketer for advice about building an audience, they will tell you the importance of posting consistency. Producing regular content is a proven way to increase your internet traffic.

Posting consistently is also a pain in the neck for a lot of small businesses (including ours at times). We have found that we are so busy creating marketing pieces for other companies that our own content marketing efforts can sometimes get tossed aside. **Consistently posting an article once a week or a few times a week can be a challenging task, but it is a task that you and I can't afford to toss aside.**

In this article, we are going to talk about the importance of consistently posting and updating your website.

Blog Posts Drive Traffic to Your Site Better Than Nearly Anything Else

I've had a number of companies contact me with services offering to drive more traffic to my website. Unless they are interested in developing content, beware of these companies. Driving traffic using a shortcut that doesn't involve developing content will cost money and usually will not result in more sales. Simply put, it is fake traffic.

I want real traffic on my site! Consistently developing content will help you to push out real information to real customers. It is simply the best way to build up an online client base for small businesses.

Hubspot did a study with staggering implications for small businesses. For businesses with 1–10 employees, they found these statistics:

- Producing 1 post per month has little effect on overall internet traffic
- Producing 2–5 posts per month typically increased traffic by about 25%
- Producing 6–10 posts per month typically increased traffic by about 50%
- Producing 11–16 posts per month typically increased traffic by 150%

Once a company reached about 300 posts, they discovered that those sites received 3.5 times more traffic than a site with 20 posts or less. The results tended to compound over time.

So, what does this information mean for your small business? For most small businesses, it means that they need to write more content...a lot more. The payoff? Your site, over time, might get 3–4 times more traffic than your competitor. As you consistently post more content, you are establishing yourself as an expert and creating a great knowledge base for the community that follows you, while spending less on pay-per-click advertising.

Creating Content Consistently Increases Leads Over Time

Increased traffic to your site will result in more leads for your business. Another study done by HubSpot found that businesses who produce more blog posts tend to also produce more leads from their websites. Here is how the study breaks down for small businesses with fewer than 10 employees:

- Producing 1 post per month had little effect on overall leads generated by the site
- Producing 2–3 posts per month increased leads by 50%
- Producing 4–5 posts per month increased leads by 100%
- Producing 6–10 posts per month increased leads by 125%
- Producing 11–16 posts per month increased leads by over 300%

Even a few blog posts per month can do a lot for generating sales on your website! **If producing leads on your website is one of your business goals, then posting more often should be a major priority for you!**

Find Your Content Sweet Spot

Now comes the question, "How many is too many?" The answer to that really depends on your industry. If you constantly inundate your readers with new posts, then they are liable to get annoyed and discontinue reading your posts. However, if you are in the information business (like a news page or a product review service), then publishing several times a day is a requirement.

One small business content marketer was publishing five days per week. He published four articles, then on Fridays he posted a cartoon. He found that his subscriber list was shrinking. So, he lost the cartoon and posted just four times per week. Restricting himself to just 16 posts per month stabilized his list and his unsubscribe level dropped by 80%.

Another industry blogger I know posts every couple of days and then compiles his posts in a newsletter that gets sent out via email about every three weeks. As he watched his statistics and interviewed his audience, he found that this cadence was about right for him.

One non-profit I know posts about once a week, sends out a corresponding email about once a week, cross-promotes their posts on social media, produces a printed newsletter once a month, and produces a podcast about every other week. That flow is hugely effective for their fund-raising efforts.

Every business is different but, to be honest, I've yet to personally run into a small business that is over-posting. You can always dial it back if your stats go down, but generally speaking, your audience is starving for more good content and will reward you with more website visits and more sales as you produce it.

Writing Blog Posts That Both Readers and Search Engines Love

People don't start small businesses unless they are experts at what they do. The main purpose of your website is to showcase your expertise and to build trust. There are a lot of reasons why people decide to start writing a blog but, in the case of small businesses, there is a twofold reason why you should consider sharing your expertise online.

Why Write Blogs

First of all, a well-written blog helps to establish you and your company as a local expert. It helps you to be seen as the best in the business. Businesses that can gain a reputation as the best in the area are able to spend less time on sales and can increase their rates.

Secondly, a well-written blog helps your business to be more easily found on the internet by various search engines. Search engines are looking for the very best sources for expert information and will reward you with visitors if you contribute your expertise to the internet by developing unique content.

Writing in order to attract an audience and writing to captivate an audience can be parallel goals, so let me offer you a few tips about how to write a blog that both showcases your expertise and helps to organically improve your ranking in search engine results over time.

Does Your Blog Post Pertain to Your Business and to Your Clients?

Say this week has been a red-hot week in politics and everyone is talking about the latest stunts our political leaders just pulled. You may be tempted to start writing about your opinions in your blog. Before you start setting your keyboard on fire, you need to ask this important question: "Does the latest news pertain to your core business?"

Let's say that you sell tuxedos and the hottest news is about the latest political fallout. If you write an opinion about your political views related to the news, your post may not be particularly helpful for driving the right kind of traffic to your site. In fact, it may even confuse a search engine and hurt your SEO scores as a result.

A search engine might be left asking, "Is this a political new site or is it a tuxedo rental site?" If the robot is confused, it could avoid your site.

However, if the political fall-out happened at a black tie event, then it would be appropriate to discuss the tuxedos the politicians were wearing while they were fighting and the dos and don'ts of formal attire at political events.

Research Keywords

Tuxedo rental websites should be about everything related to tuxedos and your blog should be tackling the hottest tuxedo news, trends, and styles. Think through all the smallest topics related to your core business and write about those topics.

A few blog ideas I brainstormed for a tuxedo shop:

- Cheap Tuxedo Rentals
- Tuxedo Styles
- White Tuxedos
- What Is a Cummerbund For?
- How to Tie a Bow Tie

You should sit down with your staff and develop dozens of ideas. Then, take those ideas and plug them into Google Trends at trends.google.com. Google Trends will tell you if people are searching for the things you think they are interested in.

After I plugged in my terms, I discovered something quite unexpected:

- The search term "How to Tie a Bow Tie" is extremely popular.
- The search term "What Is a Cummerbund For?" is not popular at all—not even worth writing about.
- White tuxedos are trending.
- The search term "Cheap Tuxedo Rentals" is not nearly as popular as I thought. It's still worth writing about, but not red-hot.

Think Before You Write

Remember how your English teacher told you to write an outline before you wrote your paper? How many of you actually did that?

It turns out that your English teacher was correct. Poorly-outlined or stream-of-consciousness blog posts are confusing to both search engines and readers.

Think about the message you are trying to communicate:

- What question are you trying to answer?
- What is the purpose of this article?

Know what you are trying to say before you try to say it.

Structure Your Blog Post Logically

Simply put, your blog post should have a clear introduction that leads into your topic, various headlines in the body of the post with no more than 150 words of text under each, and a conclusion that summarizes the most important ideas that you just stated.

An example from Ties.com:

For our bow tie topic, look at this blog post from Ties.com.

- There is a clear headline explaining what the article is about: "How to Tie a Bow Tie."
- They included a video up top. That's a nice touch.
- They placed a secondary headline with the key term: "Bow Tie."
- They wrote an introductory paragraph with the key term "bow tie" as the 2nd and 3rd words in the sentence. Several synonyms for "bow tie" and "knots" are written throughout the paragraph. Google will have no trouble identifying the topic here.
- They included clear subheadings and wrote step-by-step instructions on tying a bow tie. Illustrations are present with their brand worked into each picture.
- I would have suggested that they write a concluding paragraph, but instead they put in a link to explore more knots with the hope of keeping people searching their site longer and establishing that Ties.com is the authoritative source for everything they need to know about ties and tie knots.

Conclusion

Writing an effective blog post for your small business will help you to get found online and established as a local expert, so long as you write about the right topics for SEO and create helpful, well-organized, and well-illustrated articles for your clients.

The 4 U's of Effective Content Marketing

Effective Content Marketing Is Tricky

This is especially true if you are marketing on social media. With so many voices, so much noise, how do I stand out? Many times, business owners spend money on ads and advertising spaces, but soon realize that although they have spent a lot of money and have seen, in some cases, impressive results, as soon as they stop spending the money, they disappear into the abyss of noise and clutter that make up these digital marketplaces.

So what is the secret of creating content that gets a person's attention?

Well, you need to remember two things: First, the foundational goal in any kind of marketing, especially content marketing, is to create content that helps build trust and confidence in you with your potential customers or clients.

"KNOW, LIKE, and TRUST" is the three-word mantra of any good marketing philosophy!

These words are not only individually powerful but they represent a flow of reality for your potential customers or clients. New customers are new because they did not KNOW you, but now they do. New clients who KNOW you will not TRUST you until they LIKE you. However, just because a potential customer or client KNOWS and LIKES you doesn't mean that they TRUST you to the point of giving you their business. What you produce in content must be reliable and the information must have integrity. It also must show the innovative side of who you are.

Why use YOUR company when other companies do the same thing that you do?

This is the essence of content marketing: As a business owner, your potential customers or clients in a digital space are still human beings. They are human beings that are exhibiting behaviors in digital spaces, but they are no less human. Human beings have certain things that are drivers for why they purchase goods or services, so the answer to the question is really based in stating what makes content interesting for the human beings that are interacting with it.

On to the 4 U's

With all that being said (and much more could be said about it, but perhaps another time), it is always good to remember the Four U's that help to differentiate content that connects with people and content that does not. These four U's are borrowed from the academic world and how research is crafted, but they are also very useful in helping us to create great marketing content.

The Four U's of Effective Content Marketing:

- **Useful:** How will this product or service benefit my customers in the current business climate?

- **Unique:** How is the product or service I offer unique compared to others that are in the marketplace? What is uniquely "mine" about it?

- **Urgent:** Why is this product or service important and why is it important to trust me? What happens if the customer does not use my company? What are the ramifications? So what?

- **Ultra-Specific:** What ultra-specific (and preferably foundational) area am I trying to market to my potential customers/clients? What makes it ultra-specific? Demographics, methodology, scientific merit, innovation to the industry, etc.?

These Four "U's" will help you write content to position your company's goods and services in a light that makes an impact on the business reality of your potential clients and customers. It is more than selling a product or service, it is about selling YOU and what makes your business stand out from the rest of the marketplace.

Dozens of Blog Post Ideas

Are you having a difficult time coming up with ideas for a blog post? We started with a list of effective blog topics that we bought from Digital Marketer. Here is our twist on some of the most popular blog post ideas out there:

Useful Blog Post Ideas

1. **List post:** Create a list of books, tools, or anything else that you might find helpful.

2. **How-To post:** Create step-by-step instructions on how to accomplish a task.

3. **Case Study post:** *(The term 'case study' carries a great deal of perceived value)* Unpack the details of a project you are working on.

4. **Problem/Solution post:** Outline a problem or a pain point that a client is facing and then address the solution you came up with.

5. **Research post:** For you academics out there, research a topic and then post your findings.

6. **FAQ post:** Post some Frequently Asked Questions you get from your customers.

7. **SAQ post:** These are "Should Ask" Questions. Post questions that you should ask a professional in your field before you hire them.

8. **Checklist post:** People love "Ultimate Checklists!" Create a checklist for accomplishing a task.

9. **Ultimate Guide post:** Create an extensive step-by-step process for a complex task. Release a few posts about it at a time, then offer the whole process in a paid download.

10. **Definition post:** Create a post that defines jargon or obscure industry terms.

11. **Series post:** Break a large topic into a series of posts. Release them once a week. Make sure to create links in the posts between various parts of the series.

12. **Stats post:** Publish some statistics that your team has gathered or observed.

Generous Blog Post Ideas

13. **Profile post:** Highlight a member of your staff or an influential person in your industry. Make sure you notify them and get their permission. Usually, they will agree and will share the post on their network too.

14. **Crowdsourced post:** Use your social media channels to ask people what they want to know from you. Create a post or a series of posts with the answer.

15. **Interview post:** Interview a local celebrity, a leader in your industry, a member of your staff, one of your favorite clients, or maybe even a national celebrity. Post the interview on your blog.

16. **Link Roundup post:** Compile a list of links to articles from other people that you appreciate. Write up an abstract for each of them and put it all together in a post.

17. **Quote post:** People love quotes from influential people. Put together a list of quotes that relate to some part of your business.

18. **Best of the Web post:** Compile a list of sites and resources that you love to go to. Write up a short description and then share those sites.

19. **Pick of the Week post:** Write up a short post that describes one site, one tool, one book, one podcast, one store, or some other resource that you love and want to share with others.

Entertaining Blog Post Ideas

20. **People to Follow post:** Curate a list of influential people in your industry. Describe them and provide links to their content.

21. **Story post:** People love great stories! Write up a post with an entertaining story that you'd like to share.

22. **Satire post:** Be humorous in the form of extreme exaggeration or satire. For some businesses, this can be dangerous, so make sure it is related to your core business and not just to your personal interests. Sports and politics are easy targets for these types of posts.

23. **Cartoon post:** Share a cartoon that relates to your core business.

24. **Meme post:** Share a series of memes that relate to your industry. Make sure to share these on social media as well.

25. **Parody post:** Exaggerate the shortcomings of a well-known person in your niche industry.

Timely Blog Post Ideas

26. **Review post:** Write up a thoughtful review of a new product released in your field.

27. **Survey post:** Choose a newsworthy or trending topic, conduct a survey using social media, and then publish the results on a post.

28. **News post:** Create content on your blog about events in your industry as they are happening.

29. **Trends post:** Research the latest trends in your industry and then publish the results.

30. **Issue post:** Choose a controversial issue in your industry, explain the controversy, and offer an opinion or an invitation for discussion.

Human Interest Blog Post Ideas

31. **Inspirational post:** Post a story, picture, or quote that inspires an emotion.

32. **Holiday post:** Deliver well-wishes to your followers on holidays throughout the year.

33. **Guard Down post:** Let your guard down and share a deeply personal experience. People will often relate to a failure, a struggle, or a painful experience you are dealing with.

34. **Behind the Scenes post:** Give people a sneak peek behind the scenes to see how things are made.

35. **Off-Topic post:** This type of post can be risky and should not be utilized often, but consider writing about a topic that interests you but that you don't address very often.

36. **Rant post:** Show your human side by expressing your passion or your anger about a certain topic. This approach does not work for everyone, but in some audiences, it is well-received.

Promotional Blog Post Ideas

37. **Comparison post:** Simply compare two products and highlight the benefits and features of each .

38. **Project Showcase post:** Take great pictures and write about a project that you are really proud of.

39. **Income Report post:** Open up the books and talk about your business finances.

40. **Company Update post:** Let your readers know about changes at your company: New hires, new products, and new opportunities they have with you.

41. **Presentation post:** Publish presentations given by yourself or your employees that contain interesting information your customers might appreciate.

42. **Best Of post:** Create a post that highlights the most popular posts on your site over the last year.

43. **Product Update post:** Did a popular product recently receive an update? Talk about its new features.

44. **Product Tip post:** Talk about ways to best use your product or service.

Conversational Blog Post Ideas

45. **What If post:** Create a post that speculates, "What would happen if..." It's best if the topic is a little debatable.

46. **Debate post:** Use your blog to present one side of a debate. Ask readers to comment with their opinions.

47. **Attack post:** Be careful with this one. Sometimes it is appropriate to pick a fight on your blog.

48. **Prediction post:** Write about trends in your industry and what you predict will be the end result of those trends.

49. **Reaction post:** Use your blog to react to something written in another blog.

Engaging Blog Post Ideas

50. **Question post:** Curate questions from your audience on social media. Answer those questions in a blog post.

51. **Challenge post:** Use a blog post to pose a challenge to your audience.

52. **Customer Showcase post:** Write up a post about a customer and how they are using your products or services.

53. **Freebie post:** Find a list of internet freebies. Write up descriptions of each and then post links in your blog.

54. **Contest post:** Put together content and announce it on your blog.

55. **Blog Post Ideas post:** Make a blog post about blog post ideas.

Using Social Media to Effectively Promote Your Website and Blog

Social Media Promotion Begins When You Socialize Your Content

Socialized content from your blog boosts web traffic and increases leads as a result.

Whether you are a business owner trying to squeeze in time for blogging, a content marketer at an agency leading the development of a client's site, or a full-time blogger writing prolifically on your own site, you should have a detailed plan and purpose for your blog.

Our goal for our social media pages is to engage with customers in order to establish our company as a trustworthy and approachable expert in our industry. I believe most businesses should have a similar goal with their social media presence.

Let's say you own a hair salon. You often post pictures on your social media pages of hairstyles you created for weddings and special events. You also occasionally post the worst hairstyles from all over the web. Your social media posts are wildly popular, but are they driving sales? Make sure that your posts are connected to your website. It is fine to be popular on Facebook, but for a business, it is better to use that popularity to invite people to make an appointment (without it sounding like a sales pitch).

Social media is an amazing tool to reach out to a wider audience as well as to build a loyal following for your business. **It usually takes time and consistency for a small business to have measurable success on social media.** Social media by itself does not drive sales as well as a social media strategy that is linked to a great website with an informative blog.

Studies on Small-Business Social Media Promotion Reveal Some Amazing Statistics

Sprout Social did a study that revealed that 75% of people who are on social media purchased items they saw advertised on social media. Additionally, a buyer is 57% more likely to buy a product from a company they own if they see it featured on their social media feed.

People are also using social media extensively to seek out product recommendations. If your customers are recommending you on social media, it would be wise to have a page they can link to on that social media platform. Social media is becoming the new standard for word-of-mouth advertising for many small businesses.

However, if you just post ads on social media without developing your page, it might prove to be a waste of time. Even worse, if you are viewed as a pushy salesman on social media, you're likely to lose followers and credibility.

Social Media Is Highly Relational

The social nature of social media pages is really good for those who are seeking to be known and trusted as experts. People can get to know you, your product, and your passion for what you do.

You can't think of social media as a traditional advertisement. It's not like a display ad in the newspaper. It is a two-way communication tool. No one really wants to have a two-way conversation with a pushy salesman. They do want to have a chat with a trusted friend and an expert in the industry.

So, here are a few tips for how your small business can be a good friend on social media.

Share Great Content

Focus on posting content your audience will find valuable. Don't talk about yourself. Talk about your client and their needs. Talk about serving them well. Offer advice, tips, tricks, special offers, insider information, unique opportunities, and recommendations that your customers might find helpful. Your posts should fall into one of the following five categories:

1. **Fascinating:** Is the information you're sharing entertaining, newsworthy, humorous, or unusual?

2. **Educational:** Does the information help people know more about what they are already interested in?

3. **Time/Money Saving:** Will the information you post help people save time or money?

4. **Inspiring:** Does your post help to improve a person's life?

5. **Status-Building:** Does the information help a person increase their wealth, knowledge, or help them be smarter?

Know Who You Are Talking To

Does your company focus mostly on business-to-business sales? Do you manufacture a product that only other businesses would be interested in buying? If so, Facebook might not be the best place to spend a lot of your time. LinkedIn is a better place to invest your promotional energy.

On the other hand, do you own a local pizza restaurant? LinkedIn might be an utter waste of your time and energy if you are trying to reach out to families.

Facebook, Instagram, Twitter, and LinkedIn all are valuable tools if they are used properly. However, if your business audience does not tend to traffic on your favorite platform, it could be a waste of time and money.

Pick Your Platform(s) Wisely

A sure-fire way to experience media burnout is by trying to keep up with too many social media platforms. If you own a small business, you can probably only engage on one social media platform well and you should not even try to post on more than three.

Make sure you do a little research for the most current trends and post on the platform that is most heavily used by your target audience:

- If your sales are mostly business-to-business, then LinkedIn is probably a good choice.
- Do you own a restaurant or offer residential services? Then Facebook and Yelp could be really great choices.
- Are teenagers typically buying your products? Instagram or TikTok might get better results for you.
- Does your product have a great visual appeal? Then consider posting beautiful photographs of it on Pinterest.

Read Your Statistics to Have a Metric for Success

Decide what constitutes success with your social media campaigns. Typically, businesses measure social media success using these two metrics: Engagement and ROI.

- **Engagement:** Are people liking, sharing, and reposting your media? Are you attracting new fans? Are the people who like your page good potential customers? Is your social media creating a community online? If your followers are engaged with your site, it helps to establish your business as an authoritative source. If you continue to reach people with your posts and quality content, eventually those people will turn into advocates for your business.

- **Return on Investment (ROI):** Statistics are continually being gathered by Facebook and your website. Look at the flow of traffic. Is your social media referring people to your website? Does a product tend to sell better when you feature it on social media? Are your special offers bringing results?

Listen to Your Audience

Simply put, ask your followers what they want to learn from you.

- Offer to answer questions
- Conduct a survey
- Ask their opinion about products you offer
- Offer to write a blog post on subjects they submit to you

Listen to what people are saying and don't continue to offer information your followers aren't interested in receiving. If you receive comments or criticism, remember to respond professionally. When you show your followers that you're listening, you'll gain more loyal followers in the end.

So, create a plan, post consistently, be social, measure your results, and listen to your followers.

Holistic SEO? What Is That?
Why Is It the Best Approach?

A Regular Blogging Program Is the Key for Success with Holistic SEO

Holistic SEO is the process of building content on your website so that you get steady, ongoing traffic from search engines like Google. Google's mission statement is this:

"We want to organize the world's information and make it universally accessible and useful."

Search engines, like Google, are looking for great content. If you create great content on your website, then search engines are more likely to draw potential customers to it.

What is Holistic Search Engine Optimization?

Search engine optimization is the process by which you can increase the quality and quantity of your website traffic.

A good holistic SEO campaign will increase the visibility of your website or a specific web page to users of web search engines. SEO is all about getting results that you do not pay for on the internet. Thus, improving your SEO does not result from the purchase of paid placement on the internet.

The Importance of Blogging

A blog is an article posted on the internet that businesses use so that potential customers can find their websites. They are also a way to provide more updated, important information to customers who visit your website regularly. If you don't write a regular blog, then you need to start typing. Well-written blogs make you look like the expert in your business that you are. They also communicate important information related to your business. Customers and potential customers will begin to follow your blogs, always looking forward to the next one you will post.

A Gold Mine Many Pass Up

The sad reality is, many business owners have gotten their feet wet in blogging, but are failing to take full advantage of the enormous marketing potential of their blogs.

A recent study by blogger.com shows that about 60% of businesses have blogs, yet 65% of those who have started blogging have not even updated their blogging program in the past year!

If you want to take advantage of the many benefits of blogging, you need to provide fresh, relevant content regularly. It is easy to understand why businesses drop their blog programs: Because there are so many time-consuming components involved in managing a business, there is no one in that business that can take the time necessary to write thoughtful blogs.

The Basics of Good SEO

First of all, good SEO begins with a great SEO plugin like what you'll find at Yoast. Yoast offers some incredible tools and training. Install the plugin and, we recommend, upgrade to the Premium service. Then, watch their training video. They will walk you through the process, make sure you are using proper keywords, and ensure that those keywords are featured in:

- The title of the blog
- Headings and subheadings
- Introductory paragraphs
- Concluding paragraphs
- Title tags and meta descriptions
- Anchor text (text you hyperlink to other related pages on your site)

When SEO is programmed properly, search engines know how to index your content and ultimately will lead to quality, organic traffic to your site.

CPSIA information can be obtained
at www.ICGtesting.com
Printed in the USA
BVHW062317251122
652777BV00009B/214